BE A ZOOKEEPER

Wendy Clemson and David Clemson

ticktock

Copyright © ticktock Entertainment Ltd 2007
First published in Great Britain in 2007 by ticktock Media Ltd.,
Unit 2, Orchard Business Centre, North Farm Road,
Tunbridge Wells, Kent, TN2 3XF

ticktock project editor: Rebecca Clunes
ticktock project designer: Sara Greasley

ISBN 978 1 84696 063 5
Printed in China
A CIP catalogue record for this book is available from the British Library.

Picture credits
t=top, b=bottom, c=centre, l-left, r=right
Ticktock Media Archive 4BL, 4TR, 8T, 15; **Alamy** 23 Jim West; **Corbis** 8B Reuters, 10-11 David Gray/Reuters, 27 Ariel
Skelley; **London Zoo** 20; **Nature Photo Library** 25TR Lynn M. Stone; **Science Photo Library** 22 Alexis Rosenfeld;
Shutterstock 1-3, 4TL, 4BR, 5, 6-7 (all), 9, 12-13 (all), 15 , 16, 17, 18-19 (all), 21, 24, 25TL, 25B, 26 (all), 28-31 (all).
All cover images are from Shutterstock.

Every effort has been made to trace the copyright holders, and we apologise in advance for any unintentional omissions.
We would be pleased to insert the appropriate acknowledgements in any subsequent edition of this publication.

Contents

Welcome to the Zoo

Today you will be helping the keepers at the City Zoo. Many of the animals at the zoo are endangered. This means there are not many of them left. Some of the animals have lost their habitat in the wild. Some of the animals are in danger from hunters. The zoo is a safe place to live.

Looking after the animals is an exciting and important job.

The zookeepers give the animals food and water.

The cages are kept interesting, with lots for the animals to do.

The zookeepers and the zoo vet help the animals if they get sick.

Zoo visitors often ask the keepers questions about the animals.

But did you know that zookeepers sometimes have to use maths?

In this book you will find lots of number puzzles that zookeepers have to solve every day. You will also get the chance to answer lots of number questions about animals.

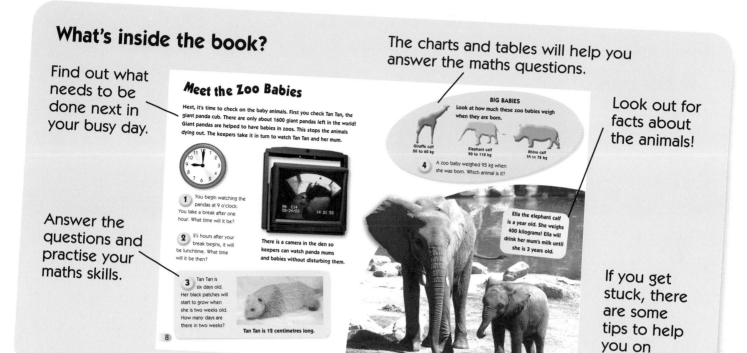

What's inside the book?

Find out what needs to be done next in your busy day.

The charts and tables will help you answer the maths questions.

Answer the questions and practise your maths skills.

Look out for facts about the animals!

If you get stuck, there are some tips to help you on pages 30-31.

Meet the Zoo Babies

Next, it's time to check on the baby animals. First you check Tan Tan, the giant panda cub. There are only about 1600 giant pandas left in the world! Giant pandas are helped to have babies in zoos. This stops the animals dying out. The keepers take it in turn to watch Tan Tan and her mum.

1 You begin watching the pandas at 9 o'clock. You take a break after one hour. What time will it be?

2 2¼ hours after your break begins, it will be lunchtime. What time will it be then?

3 Tan Tan is six days old. Her black patches will start to grow when she is two weeks old. How many days are there in two weeks?

There is a camera in the den so keepers can watch panda mums and babies without disturbing them.

Tan Tan is 12 centimetres long.

8

BIG BABIES

Look at how much these zoo babies weigh when they are born.

Giraffe calf 50 to 60 kg

Elephant calf 90 to 110 kg

Rhino calf 35 to 75 kg

4 A zoo baby weighed 95 kg when she was born. Which animal is it?

Ella the elephant calf is a year old. She weighs 400 kilograms! Ella will drink her mum's milk until she is 3 years old.

9

Ready to be a zookeeper for the day?

You will need paper, a pencil, a ruler and don't forget to wear your wellies! Let's go...

Time to Check the Animals

Your day starts at 8 o'clock. Your first job is to check all the animals are well. If an animal is sick or hurt, the zookeeper must tell the zoo vet right away. You can use this map of part of the zoo to find your way around.

Answer these questions using the zoo map.

1 You walk past the cafe, the giraffes, the bird house and the big cats. Are you walking clockwise or anti-clockwise?

2 The giraffes are to the south of the cafe. What is directly to the west?

3 How many right angle turns do you make if you walk the length of the red path?

ZOO MAP

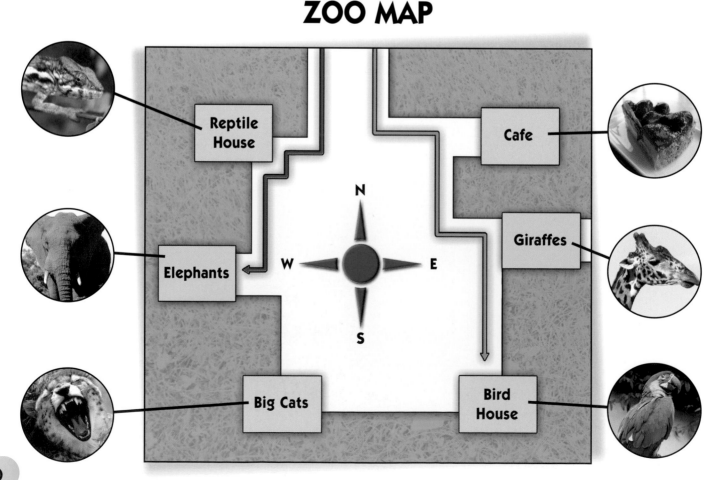

Reptile House

Cafe

N

Giraffes

W — E

Elephants

S

Big Cats

Bird House

4 Next, you check the warthogs. Warty is waiting for his breakfast! Warty is 18 years old – that's very old for a warthog! What is the difference between your age and Warty's age?

In the wild, warthogs eat grass, berries, tree bark and dead animals. In the zoo they eat food pellets and vegetables.

WARTHOG TUSKS

Warthogs have four tusks. Warty's tusks are 20 cm long. Use a ruler to measure this line.

5 How much shorter is the line than Warty's tusk?

Meet the Zoo Babies

Next, it's time to check on the baby animals. First you check Tan Tan, the giant panda cub. There are only about 1600 giant pandas left in the world! Giant pandas are helped to have babies in zoos. This stops the animals dying out. The keepers take it in turn to watch Tan Tan and her mum.

1 You begin watching the pandas at 9 o'clock. You take a break after one hour. What time will it be?

2 2½ hours after your break begins, it will be lunchtime. What time will it be then?

There is a camera in the den so keepers can watch panda mums and babies without disturbing them.

3 Tan Tan is six days old. Her black patches will start to grow when she is two weeks old. How many days are there in two weeks?

Tan Tan is 12 centimetres long.

BIG BABIES

Look at how much these zoo babies weigh when they are born.

Giraffe calf
50 to 60 kg

Elephant calf
90 to 110 kg

Rhino calf
35 to 75 kg

4 A zoo baby weighed 95 kg when she was born. Which animal is it?

Ella the elephant calf is a year old. She weighs 400 kilograms! Ella will drink her mum's milk until she is 3 years old.

Kimba the Baby Kangaroo

Sometimes animal mums don't know how to care for their babies, or the animal mums get ill. When this happens the keepers have to raise the babies by hand. Kimba's mum is ill, so the keepers are caring for him. He needs four bottles of milk a day. It's your turn to give Kimba his bottle!

FEEDING KIMBA

Kimba is fed special kangaroo milk. To make it, you must add 1 spoonful of milk powder for every 50 millilitres of water.

1 How many spoonfuls of milk powder do you add to this bottle?

150 ml

2 How many spoonfuls will you use in this bottle?

250 ml

KIMBA'S WEIGHT

Zookeepers weigh animal babies regularly. They check the babies are healthy and growing properly.

3 When Kimba was 4 months old, he weighed this much. What was his weight at 4 months?

4 Kimba was weighed again at 6 months. How heavy was he then?

5 Kimba is now eight months old, but he will need bottles for another six months. Can you do these puzzles using the numbers 6 and 8?

6 + 8

8 + 8

8 – 6

6 + 6

Here is Kimba aged 8 months. He now weighs 4½ kilograms.

Today's Delivery of Food

It's time to visit the food warehouse. The zoo animals are fed fresh food like meat and vegetables. They also eat special pellets that give them the same vitamins as the food they eat in the wild. A truck has just arrived. The truck is delivering carrots and mangoes.

1 What weight of carrots is the truck carrying?

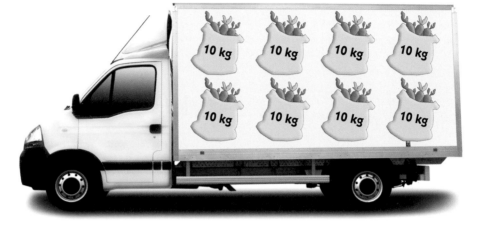

2 If the truck looked like this, what weight of carrots would it be carrying?

3 There are 2 kilograms of mangoes in a box. What is the weight in 7 boxes?

The chimpanzees love mangoes!

FOOD CHART

Some animals only eat plants. They eat leaves, grass, fruit or vegetables. Other animals are meat-eaters. They feed on insects, birds, fish or mammals. Some animals eat plants and meat.

4 An animal name is missing from the bottom of this chart. Which of these three animals is the missing one?

- The tiger, which eats other animals.
- The anteater, which eats insects and fruit.
- The deer, which eats leaves and grass.

Animal	Plant eaters	Meat eaters
Otter		✔
Bear	✔	✔
Hippo	✔	
?	✔	✔

5 This zebra is given 1 sack of hay and ½ a bag of pellets at each meal. She is fed twice a day. How much does she eat a day?

Lunch for the Orangutans

It is time to give the orangutans their lunch of fruit. Orangutans live in rainforests. They spend all day looking for food. At the zoo, their food is spread around their cage, and put in different places every day. The orangutans have to look for it, just like they would in the wild.

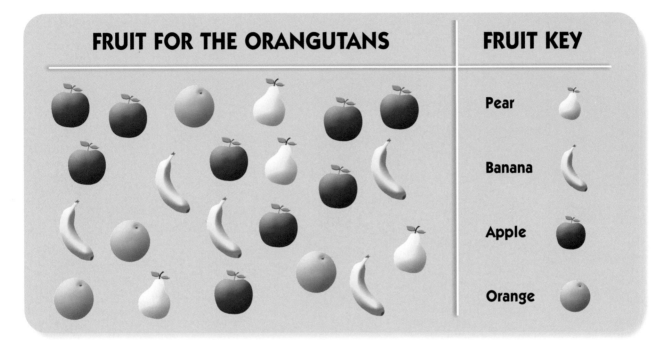

FRUIT FOR THE ORANGUTANS

FRUIT KEY

Pear

Banana

Apple

Orange

1 This picture shows the fruit given to the orangutans. How many pears are there?

2 There are more bananas than oranges. Is this true or false?

3 Count the number of apples. Is this an odd number or an even number?

4 Look at the numbers below. Can you pick out all of the odd numbers?

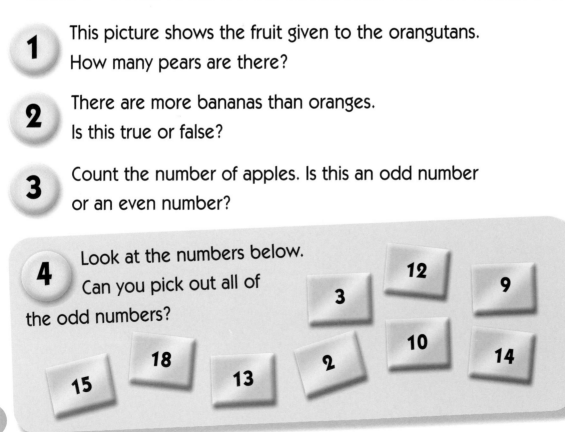

12 9 3 15 18 13 2 10 14

5 Bella the baby orangutan is 18 months old. How old is Bella in years?

6 Bella's friend Chang is 24 months old. How old is he in years?

Bella's mum is called Cindy. She is 23 years old.

Bella

Chang

Snakes and Birds

It's 2 o'clock. Time to help the snake keeper give a talk to the visitors. The visitors are allowed to stroke the boa constrictor. Its skin feels very smooth and dry. The keeper says that she feeds the snake on rats and chicks.

THE ZOO'S LONGEST SNAKES

Cobra 6 metres

Python 10 metres

Rattlesnake 2½ metres

Boa Constrictor 5 metres

Anaconda 8 metres

1 The boa constrictor isn't the zoo's longest snake. Which snake is the longest?

2 Which snake is half the length of the python?

3 How many snakes are shorter than the cobra?

THE ZOO'S OLDEST BIRDS

Lovebird
18 years

Macaw
50 years

Canary
12 years

Cockatoo
62 years

At the bird house, Charlie the macaw says "Hello" to the visitors. Macaws can copy words they hear. They repeat words again and again.

4 Can you put the birds in the chart in order, from the youngest bird to the oldest?

COUNTING THE BIRDS

The keepers have a chart to show how many birds are in the bird house.

Bird	Number in zoo
Lovebirds	16
Macaws	4
Canaries	9
Cockatoos	27

5 How many canaries are there?

6 What sort of bird does the zoo have fewest of?

7 What sort of bird does the zoo have most of?

The Playful Penguins

You check on the penguins next. The zoo has several sorts of penguin in the same cage. The eight Magellanic penguins are the newest. They arrived from a nearby zoo last week. They look as if they are settling in well at their new home.

TYPES OF PENGUIN

| Magellanic penguin | Chinstrap penguin | King penguin | Gentoo penguin |

Penguins usually swim at about 13 kilometres per hour, twice as fast as a good human swimmer.

1 King penguins are 90 centimetres tall. Magellanic penguins are about 20 centimetres shorter than this. How tall are Magellanic penguins?

2 Chinstrap penguins are about 15 centimetres shorter than King penguins. How tall is that?

3 The smallest adult Gentoo is about the size of a Chinstrap penguin. The largest is about the size of a King penguin. What is the range of heights Gentoo penguins can be?

These are Magellanic penguins. In the wild they live about 25 years, but in zoos they can live as long as 30 years.

WHERE ARE THEY?

The zoo has 100 penguins. Some are in the pool, some are on the rocks and some are in their den.

4 There are 70 penguins on the rocks and 5 in the pool. How many are in the den?

5 There are 25 penguins in the pool and 20 in the den. How many on the rocks?

Mucking Out the Giraffes

Oh no! It's time to clean out the giraffes' pen. This is probably the worst part of your job. You sweep up the dirty straw and giraffe dung and pile it into the wheelbarrow. Then you spread fresh clean straw out. That's better!

1 It takes four keepers 1 hour to clean the giraffe's pen. How long would it take two keepers?

> Giraffes eat 35 kilograms of food every day. In the zoo they are fed leaves, hay and carrots.

A POO PICTOGRAM!

This shows the number of buckets of poo collected from some animal pens.

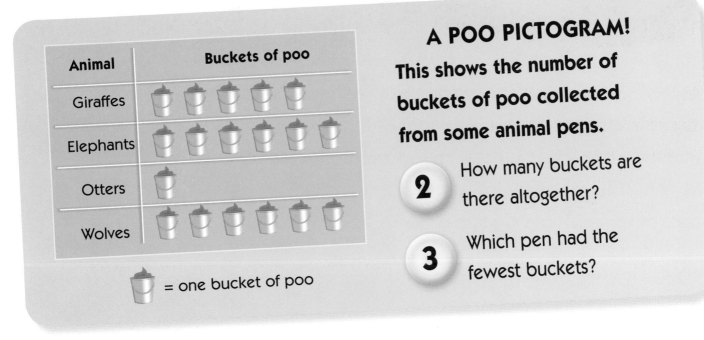

Animal	Buckets of poo
Giraffes	
Elephants	
Otters	
Wolves	

 = one bucket of poo

2 How many buckets are there altogether?

3 Which pen had the fewest buckets?

4 Straw comes in bales. How many bales are in these piles?

A B C

STRAW SHAPES

5 Some bales of straw have been pushed together. When you look down on them you see new shapes. How many sides does each of these new shapes have?

6 Can you name these new shapes?

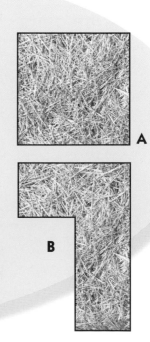

A

B

Staying Healthy

At 3 o'clock you call the vet because you're worried about one of the turtles. He is not diving under the water like the other turtles. You know this is a sign that he is ill. The vet gives the turtle medicine. Then you ask the vet to check the tiger cub, which has been limping.

TURTLE MEDICINE

A

B

C

These syringes contain different amounts of the turtle's medicine. Can you answer the questions below?

This turtle has not been eating. He is given antibiotics.

1 How much medicine is there in each of the syringes?

2 The turtle needs 10 ml of medicine. The vet uses two of the syringes. Which two does she use?

The vet checks the tiger cub's paws. A tiger's claws are retractable – they can be pulled inside the paws, just like a house cat's claws.

3 Tigers have five claws on each of their front paws, and four claws on each of their back paws. How many claws do they have altogether?

4 The tiger cub needs some vitamins. He is given two pills a day. How many days until the pills in the bottle are all used up?

20 pills

The Night House

Your next visit is to the Night House. You step inside and wait for your eyes to get used to the dark. This is where the nocturnal animals live. Nocturnal animals sleep in the day and wake up at night to look for food. The Night House is dark so they think it is night time.

In the zoo, the fruit bats are fed figs, oranges, pears, grapes and watermelon.

BAT CHART

The bats should be awake during the day, so visitors can see them. Do you think they are? You decide to watch them to find out.

1 How many bats were awake at 3pm?

2 What time was it when the greatest number of bats were awake?

3 How many more bats were awake at 9am than were awake at midnight?

Time of day	Number of bats awake
9am	32
Midday	41
3pm	27
Midnight	2

4 Visitors like to know about the animals they see, so each pen has some information about the animals inside. Unfortunately, the labels have fallen off two of the pens in the Night House. Can you decide which facts should go with each animal? You know that:

• the tarsier is longer than the aye-aye.

• one of the animals has a tail that is twice as long as its body.

Tarsier

• from Asia

Aye-Aye

• from Madagascar in Africa

• body about 15 centimetres long

• body about 35 centimetres long

• tail about 50 centimetres long

• tail about 30 centimetres long

Like most nocturnal animals, this bushbaby has big eyes to help it see in the dark.

25

The Children's Corner

It's getting late, but there are still lots of visitors in the Children's Corner. In this part of the zoo, some of the tamer animals are kept in one big pen. Children can go into the pen and stroke the animals. You warn the visitors that the zoo will be closing soon.

CHILDREN'S CORNER HUNDRED CHART

1	2	3	4	5	6	7	8	9	10
11		13		15					
	22	23							
								39	
				46					
									60
			64						
			75						
81							88		
						97			

Look at this hundred chart. Can you answer the questions on the next page?

Sometimes, visitors are allowed to feed the animals in the Children's Corner.

Can you name these animals?

 1 **Animal A** I am on square 83.

 2 **Animal B** I am on a square that is 3 tens and 2 ones.

 3 On which number is there a donkey?

 4 How many rabbits are there in the hundred square?

 5 How many squares have children on them?

The Zoo Shop

There's only 10 minutes until the zoo closes. You just have time to go to the zoo shop to buy your friend a present. The shop is very important to the zoo. It raises money to help pay for looking after the animals.

1 The tiger posters cost £2.50 each. You have £5 so how many could you buy?

2 If you had £10 how many posters could you buy?

JIGSAW OR BOOK?

JAGUAR JIGSAW 100 pieces!

50p + 50p + 50p

£1 + £1 + 50p + 20p + 5p

3 How much does the jigsaw cost?

4 How much does the book cost?

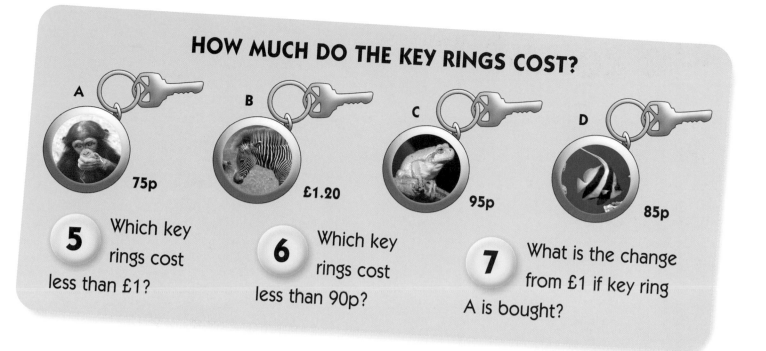

HOW MUCH DO THE KEY RINGS COST?

A **75p**

B **£1.20**

C **95p**

D **85p**

5 Which key rings cost less than £1?

6 Which key rings cost less than 90p?

7 What is the change from £1 if key ring A is bought?

Your day at the zoo is over. You need to rest, and so do the animals. It will be another busy day tomorrow.

Tips and Help

PAGES 6-7

Clockwise – Clockwise is the way the hands of a clock move around.
Anti-clockwise – is the other way around.

Right angle – There are four right angles in a complete turn. A right angle is often shown like this:

right angle

PAGES 8-9

Telling the time – The shorter hand is the hour hand (It tells us what o'clock). The longer hand is the minute hand. It shows how many minutes to or past the hour (o'clock).
A week – There are seven days in a week.

PAGES 10-11

Adding up – Remember you can add numbers in any order. So the sum of 8 and 6 is the same as the sum of 6 and 8.
Subtracting (Taking away) – It is important to put the bigger number first: 8–6 gives the answer 2.

PAGES 12-13

Counting in tens – It is useful to be able to count in tens from 0 to 100. The pattern is 0 10 20 30 40 50 60 70 80 90 100. Can you count back in tens also?

Chart – A chart is a clear way to compare at least two kinds of information. The chart shows that the missing animal eats both plants and meat. Which animal eats plants such as fruit, and meat such as insects?

PAGES 14-15

Odds and evens – Even numbers are in the pattern of counting in twos: 2 4 6 8 and so on. Odd numbers are those that are not even: 1 3 5 7 and so on. Try counting the pattern of twos up to 20. Now try the odds from 1 to 19.

A Year – There are 12 months in a year. You have a birthday when you become a year older. Bella has had her first birthday.

PAGES 16-17

Putting numbers in order – The smallest whole numbers have no tens (only ones or units). They are the numbers 1 2 3 4 5 6 7 8 9. Next look for numbers with only 1 ten (like 12) and put the number with fewest units first, then the others. Then see if there is a number with more than 1 ten.

PAGES 18-19

A Range – Here this tells us the smallest a measure can be and the largest a measure can be.

Making 100 – To find a missing number start by adding together the numbers you are given and then take the total away from 100.

PAGES 20-21

Side – In maths a flat shape is said to have 'sides'. This rectangle has 4 sides. The hexagon has 6 sides.

rectangle   hexagon

PAGES 22-23

Scale – In maths, scales help us 'read off' measures. Check what measure is shown. For example a ruler shows us centimetres. These syringes show millilitres.

Counting in twos – Count aloud: 2 4 6 8 10 12 14 16 18 20. Each number means a day's pills so we can work out how many days' supply we have.

PAGES 24-25

Daytime – 9am, midday and 3pm are all times during the day. Midnight is a time during the night.

Twice – This means x2. So 'twice as long as' means 'two times as long as'.

PAGES 26-27

A Hundred Square – This is a square made of ten rows each of ten numbers. It goes from 1 to 100 in that order. It is a good way to set out the first hundred numbers because you can use it to find lots of patterns.

PAGES 28-29

Pounds and pence – Remember one pound and twenty pence can be written as £1.20 We use the 'dot' between the 1 and the 2 to separate the pounds and pence.

Answers

PAGES 6-7

1 clockwise
2 reptile house
3 5
4 if you are 5 the answer is 13
  if you are 6 the answer is 12
  if you are 7 the answer is 11
  if you are 8 the answer is 10
  if you are 9 the answer is 9
  if you are 10 the answer is 8
5 10 centimetres

PAGES 8-9

1 10 o'clock
2 12:30 or half past twelve
3 14 days
4 elephant calf

PAGES 10-11

1 3 spoonfuls
2 5 spoonfuls
3 ½ kg
4 1½ kg
5 6 + 8 = 14
  8 − 6 = 2
  8 + 8 = 16
  6 + 6 = 12

PAGES 12-13

1 80 kg
2 160 kg
3 14 kg
4 anteater
5 2 sacks of hay and 1 bag of pellets

PAGES 14-15

1 4 pears
2 true – there are more bananas
3 9 apples – this is an odd number
4 3, 9, 13 and 15
5 1½ years
6 2 years

PAGES 16-17

1 python
2 boa constrictor
3 2
4 canary, lovebird
   macaw, cockatoo
5 9
6 macaws
7 cockatoos

PAGES 18-19

1 70 centimetres
2 75 centimetres
3 75–90 centimetres
4 25 in the den
5 55 on the rocks

PAGES 20-21

1 2 hours
2 18 buckets
3 otter pen
4 A 3 bales
  B 5 bales
  C 4 bales
5 A 4 sides
  B 6 sides
6 A square
  B hexagon

PAGES 22-23

1 A 6 ml
  B 2 ml
  C 8 ml
2 B and C
3 18 claws
4 10 days

PAGES 24-25

1 27 bats
2 midday
3 30 bats
4 The tarsier is 35 cm long with a tail of 50 cm. The aye-aye is 15 cm long with a tail of 30 cm.

PAGES 26-27

1 duck
2 pig
3 square 50
4 7 rabbits
5 17 squares

PAGES 28-29

1 2 posters
2 4 posters
3 £1.50
4 £2.75
5 A, C and D
6 A
7 25p